THE
BENEFIT
OF
FARTING
EXPLAIN'D

Front cover
The Reverend Jonathan Swift by Charles Jervas. Oil painting in the National Portrait Gallery, St Martin's Place, London. "By Courtesy of the National Portrait Gallery, London".

The BENEFIT of FARTING

EXPLAIN'D:

OR, THE

FUNDAMENT-all *CAUSE*

OF THE

Diſtempers incident to the Fair Sex

By *Obadiah Fizle*, Groom of the Stool to the Princeſs
of *Arſe-Mini* in *Sardinia*.

Printed for *A. Moore*, near St. *Paul's, London*. Price 3 *d*.
or 20 *s. per* Hundred to thoſe Ladies who would
encourage this Undertaking. 1722

First published by Old Abbey Press in 1996.

Published by Old Abbey Press 1996.
10 Earl Richards Road North, Exeter, England, EX2 6AG.
Telephone/Fax 01392 72116

ISBN 0 9525179 1 4

Preface

The Reverend Jonathan Swift D.D.

Jonathan Swift was born on 30 November 1667 in Dublin, Ireland, of English parents. His father died a few months before he was born, and at the age of six his mother went back to England leaving Jonathan at Kilkenny School, Dublin. He later went on to study theology at Trinity College, Dublin. After graduating he went to London to work for Sir William Temple as a secretary. It was during this time that he started to write poetry. Eventually he returned to Ireland and entered the Church as a priest in Kilroot near Belfast, although he spent long periods in England. In 1696/7 he wrote the satire *A Tale of a Tub*. He had a close friendship with Esther Johnson (Stella) which lasted until she died in 1728. In politics he supported the Whigs but later changed to supporting the Tories when they adopted a more sympathetic attitude to the Anglican Church of Ireland. In 1713 he was appointed Dean of St Patrick's Cathedral, Dublin. It was at this time that Swift started to write political pamphlets, and other humorous pamphlets such as *The Benefit of Farting Explain'd*. In 1726 his most famous book was published, as a satirical book for adults. It was called *Gulliver's Travels*. It eventually became a well-loved children's book. In his later years he was a philanthropist, giving most of his money away. Jonathan Swift died in 1745, aged seventy-eight years, and was buried next to Stella in St Patrick's Cathedral, Dublin.

Note: The letter ſ in this publication has a horizontal bar only on the left of the letter and is known as the "long s" indicating a longer stronger s. It should not be confused with the letter f. It is only found in early books, and its use died out in the late eighteenth century. The "long s" is a variant of the lower case s (roman form ſ and italic form ſ) in initial and medial positions but not final positions in words.

This is an exact reproduction of the 1722 edition of *The Benefit of Farting Explain'd*.

Clive Davies, Exeter, England, 1996.

The Reverend Jonathan Swift by Charles Jervas. Oil painting in the National Portrait Gallery, St Martin's Place London. "By Courtesy of the National Portrait Gallery, London".

THE
BENEFIT
OF
FARTING
EXPLAIN'D

The BENEFIT of

FARTING

EXPLAIN'D:

OR, THE

FUNDAMENT-all *CAUSE*

OF THE

Diſtempers incident to the Fair Sex

Inquir'd into:

Proving *à poſteriori* moſt of the *Diſordures* in-*tail'd* on 'em are owing to *Flatulencies* not *ſeaſonably vented*.

Wrote in *Spaniſh*, by Don *Fart in hando Puff-in dorſt*, Profeſſor of *Bumbaſt* in the Univerſity of *Craccow*.

AND

Tranſlated into *Engliſh*, at the Requeſt and for the Uſe of the Lady *Damp-Fart*, of *Her-fart-ſhire*.

By *Obadiah Fizle*, Groom of the Stool to the Princeſs of *Arſe-Mini* in *Sardinia*.

A FART, though wholſome does not fail,
If barr'd of Paſſage by the Tail,
To fly back to the Head again,
And by its Fumes diſturb the Brain:
  Thus Gun-powder confin'd, you know Sir,
  Grows ſtronger, as 'tis ramm'd the cloſer;
  But, if in open Air it fires,
  In harmleſs Smoke its Force expires.

POSTSCRIPT

BY WAY OF

PREFACE

Venti indignantes magno cum Murmure Ventris,
Circum Clauſtra fremunt, media ſedet Æbolus Arce.
                                    Virgil Æneid. lib. I.

*IBERTY and Property, are the two great Bleſſings,*
every Britiſh *Subject claims, as his Birth-right*; *why Mr.*
Breech *ſhould be denied this Benefit, I ſee no Reaſon,*
but his Shame-facedneſs to appear in his own Behalf. 'Tis
true, he always ſat in the Houſe of Commons, *being at*
all Elections unanimouſly choſe as Repreſentative for the
Burrough of Rump-fort, *but thro' Modeſty was ever obſerv'd to keep* behind
Backs : *He never* open'd *his Mouth in the Houſe, but all the Members round*
nos'd *him, and took* Snuff *at every thing he* offer'd, *becauſe 'twas ſaid, that in*
his younger Days, he had been a Button-maker (*though falſely*), *for I*
remember him from his Youth, to have been a Wind-Merchant, *which he*
vented by Hole-Sail *and* re-Tail. *This Uſage put him under a conſtraint of*
being Silent, tho' he often grumbled inwardly *for it.*

  He had two Sons ; Sir Reverence, *being the Younger, was Knighted*
by K. James; *the other was a* Noiſy, Rattling, Cracking *Fellow: He*
                                                                applied

POSTSCRIPT, &c.

applied himself to the Practice of Musick *and* Phyz-ick, *and was particularly famous for the Cure of the* Wind-CHoleick, *but none ever relish'd his Musical Performance. He married into the Family of the* Swifts, *and was so active in Running, that none could ever catch him, if he once got the Start.*

Beside these two, there was another Foisted *on him, but believing him to be illegitimate, he was ashamed to own him ; he died young, and therefore made no* Noise *in the World.*

This Mr. Breech, *the Father of these, was a Man of a good* Report, *tho' some are so malicious to say, he us'd to play at* FAST *and* LOOSE ; *he was sometimes sickly, which was imputed to his being formerly bit by a* Tarantula, *because he was always observed to be relieved by the playing of a* Bag-pipe.

The hole *History of his Life and Actions, has been lately published by a* Learned and Reverend Doctor, *wherein he makes him the Eighth* Wonder of the World, *and by way of Excellency over the other Seven, has stil'd him, the Most Wonderful of them all; and tho' he endeavour'd to conceal him under the dark Veil of an* Enigma, *yet we quickly* smelt *out his* Hole *Meaning.* Tom Punsbi *who first taught him his* Ars in presenti, *was often very* Smart *upon him with his* Puns, *and he could* digest *every thing but that ;* Tom *never looked him in the Face, but he made him tremble ; they never met but Blows ensued, but* Tom *was always sure to come off Conqueror ; but notwithstanding,* Tom *made a Convert of him, and* instilled *into him the Principles of* Passive Obedience.

Now the Design of the following Essay, *is to obtain Liberty for him to* vent *his* Scent-iments *freely, and that he may be* Heard *without Offence and not be* bound *to keep Silence ; since such a Freedom will prove so serviceable to the* Fair Sex. *If I have* HANDLED THE SUBJECT *to their good Liking, I hope they'll will loudly* Crack *of the Benefit received, and That I shall judge a sufficient Reward for all my Trouble, who am*

their most Humble Servant,

FART-IN-HAND-O PUFF-INDORST.

THE

THE
Benefit of *FARTING*
EXPLAIN'D

Si fartus Venter Crepitu *luctante laborat,*
Ars te sanabit, vento Spiracula dando.
Flatum ne retine ; propellito fortiter Hostem.
Rumbulus, & Ructus, Crepitus, Strepitusq; *juvabunt.*

English't thus, for the *Benefit* of the Ladies.

If you 're opprest by rumbling Wind,
Strain hard, to squeeze it out behind.
From Puffs, and crackling Farts *Relief you'll find.*

 T has been observed of late Years, since the primitive wholsome Custom of *Toast* and *Nutmeg* in a Morning has been superseded by that pernicious Practice of *Tea* and *Coffee*, that a numberless Train of Distempers, scarce known to our Forefathers, as Spleen, Vapours, Hips, &c. have become as universal among us as the SmallPox ; the Weight of which has fallen chiefly on the Fair Sex, for Reasons I shall give hereafter. I wou'd not on any score be thought Guilty of a Design, to run down those pleasant Liquors, or derogate the least Tittle, from their due Praise, since I should thereby cause the Ladies to level the whole *Artillery* of their Resentment against me ; but must say this in their Favour, That in the first place, they serve as an Amusement, to divert two or three Hours, that would otherwise lie very heavy on their Hands in a Morning; and Secondly, to purge off that sharp corroding

Humour

Humour call'd Scandal which elſe (if too long retained) might ulcerate their Memory ; and, Thirdly, it promotes a free Circulation of Intelligence, which, they'd have no other Opportunity of coming at, being debar'd the Benefit of going to Coffee-houſes or the Exchange. But, as the greateſt Bleſſings are ſometimes attended with ſome Inconveniency, Wine that makes our Heart glad, can alſo rob us of our Reaſon ; ſo theſe moſt wholſome and pleaſing Liquors, may if not us'd with Caution produce ill Conſequences, the Prevention of which for the Benefit of that Sex, is the Deſign of this Eſſay. As in ſipping up theſe Liquors Hot, there is commonly as much *Wind as Water* ſucked in, which thro' Modeſty being debar'd a Paſſage downwardly, when Nature offers, recoils up into the Bowels, Stomach and Head, and there occaſions all thoſe dreadful Symptoms uſually aſcribed to the *Vapours* ; all which one ſeaſonable F A R T might have prevented. It has likewiſe been aſſigned as the firſt Cauſe of Quakeriſm, and Enthuſiaſm, as *Hudibras* obſerves.

> *As Wind in Hypochondria pent,*
> *Is but a F A R T, if downward ſent ;*
> *But if ſuppreſt, it upward flies,*
> *And vents itſelf in Prophecies.*

    I ſhall therefore in the firſt place, enquire into the *Nature* and *Eſſence* of a F A R T.
    Secondly, Shew the ill Conſequences of ſuppreſſing it.
    Thirdly, Prove the Lawfulneſs of it. And
    Fourthly, and *Laſtly*, Shew the many Advantages will attend an Act of Toleration or free Liberty that way.

    Firſt. It is a Queſtion greatly controverted among the Learned, Whether a F A R T be a ſpiritual or a material Subſtance ? The Profeſſors of MetaPhyz-icks have argued warmly for its Spirituality ; but the Naturaliſts as ſtrongly oppoſe them. The famous Mr. *Boyle* brings it in as an Example to prove the vaſt Subtility of Matter, ſince a F A R T, which in the *Hydroſtatical* Ballance does not weigh the Thouſandth part of a Grain, ſhall, in one Minute, expand itſelf ſo far, as to occupy the whole Atmoſphere of a large Drawing Room.
    The *Chymiſts* endeavour'd to enquire into its Nature, by reſolving it into its firſt Principles, but they ever found it as Volatile, and as hard to fix as *Mercury*, they all allow it to abound much in a volatile Sulphur, which they infer, from the briſk Senſation, wherewith it affects the

Organs

Organs of Smelling, and from its burning *Blew*, as has been found by Experiment.

Cartefius begs it as a Principle for his Philofophy, and to make it relifh the better, new chriftened it, by the name of *Materia Subtilis*, and cooking up his Syftem to the *French* Tafte, he concluded fo favoury an ingredient would pleafe their Palate, but it proved as unlucky a Material, as the Salt-peter in the Fryar's Compofition, that firft difcover'd *Gunpowder*; for taking *Vent*, it *Blew* up his whole Syftem, and exploded all his Philofophy.

The *Mathematicians* fteer'd a middle Courfe between the Naturalifts and the MetaPhiz-icians ; they own'd a F A R T to be a Quantity yet In[di]vifible, and gave it the Name of a Mathematical Point, as having neither *Length, Breadth* nor *Thicknefs*.

I therefore define a F A R T to be, " A Nitro-aerial Vapour, ex-
" hal'd from an adjacent Pond of Stagnant Water of a Saline Na-
" ture, and rarified and fublimed into the Nofe of a Microcofmical
" Alembic, by the gentle Heat of a STERCORARIOUS Balne-
" um, with a ftrong Empyreuma, and forc'd through the Pofteriours
" by the Compreffive Power of the expulfive Faculty.

Secondly,   Having explained the Nature and Effence of a F A R T, I fhall next enquire into the ill Confequences of fuppreffing it, which are almoft obvious to every one's Experience ; for in its Retrogradation, it caufes CHOLICKS, HYSTERICKS, RUMBLINGS, BELCHING, SPLEEN, *&c.* but in Women of a more ftrong Conftitution, it vents itfelf intirely in Talkativenefs ; hence we have a Reafon, why Women are more Talkative than Men ; for as the Poet obferves,

> ' Words own Wind to be their Mother,
> ' Which ftop't at one end, burft out at t'other.

Hence comes the ufual Saying, *Tell a Tale, or let a F A R T*; implying the Neceffity of Vent, one Way or t'other.

The remarkable Taciturnity of the late Widow FARTWELL, is a convincing Proof of this Doctrine ; for having her Pofteriours much dilated and relaxed by a too frequent Ufe of Clyfters in her Younger Days, was fo debilitated in her retentive Faculty, that her Wind paffing too freely that Way, there wanted a fufficient Supply to fet the Wind-Mill of her Tongue a going.

The frequent Fitts of Laughing and Crying, without any fenfible Caufe, (Symptoms common to fuch as are troubled with the Vapours)

are plainly accountable from this Suppreffion; for the Windy Vapour getting into the Mufcles that affift in Laughing, inflates them, and occafions their Laughing; but if this Vapour, when rais'd to the Head, is there condenfed by a cold melancholy Conftitution, it diftils thro' the Eyes in Form of Tears.

Thirdly, As for the Lawfulnefs of F A R T I N G none I hope will difpute that Point with me, till they fhew me a Law againft it, which I am fatisfied they can't do; and, Where there is no Law, there can be no Tranfgreffion. The *Cannon Law* (if I miftake not) is loudly for it, and the Law of Nature feems to be of our Side, and tho' it feems to be againft the Civil Law, yet the Severity of that Law was provided againft, by King *James* the firft; for a Gentleman dying by Suppreffing a F A R T in his Prefence, the King had immediately wrote over the Gate in Capital Letters this Infcription,

HERE ALL FARTS ARE FREE.

And *Cambden* obferves the Antient Efteem F A R T S were in, by Lands held by one *Baldwin* (*le Pettour*, i.e. the *FARTER*) at *Hemingfton* in *Suffolk*, by the Tenure of coming into Court on a certain Day, performing *Saltus, Sufflatus,* & *Bumbulus*, i.e. Capering, Puffing, and F A R T I N G. *Cambd.* p. 464. Its being contrary to Cuftom is no Plea, fince the fame Authority which introduced HOOP'D PETTICOATS can alfo bring FARTING in Fafhion; and there wants nothing more to make it pafs current, than fome celebrated Toaft of the Town to begin an Example. We are very forward in imitating our Neighbouring Nations in their Fafhion and Drefs, tho' never fo ridiculous, but *Back*-ward in this Point, which would be much more for our Advantage: For a F*art* is a Freeman in all the Towns *Corporate* thro' *Holland. Yfro Blowza Van Funck*, a Burgomafter's Wife of *Rotterdam*, values her felf as much upon the good *Report* of her *Bum-Battery*, as one of Our Ladies would for a fweet Voice, or an agreeable Lifp, and is as induftrious in fhewing her Performance that Way, as the other in fhewing a white Hand, a rich Ring, or a neat Snuff-Box. And the Ladies in *France* maintain, that a promifcuous Converfation on a Bog-Houfe, favours as little of Impudence or Impiety as over a Tea-Table.

Having proved the Lawfulnefs of F A R T I N G, and the ill Confequence of fuppreffing it, I fhall proceed, *Fourthly,* To fet down the Advantages the Ladies, are likely to reap by an unlimited Freedom that Way.

Way. For firft, it frees them from that long-winded Catalogue of Diftempers already mentioned, and prov'd to proceed from this Caufe, which Benefit alone were fufficient to recommend it to all thofe who value their Health; but befides this, 'twill render *Peas-Porridge* as wholefome as *Ginger-bread*, and Bottl'd *Cyder* as innocent as *Ratafia*; 'twill alfo lower the Price of *Daffy's* Elixir, and fave them a vaft yearly Expence in *Arf-a-Fœtida*, and Spirits of *Harts-Horn*, to guard them from the *Vapours*, fince hereby they become their own *Apothecaries*, to prepare a Medicine will twitch them by the *Nofe* every whit as well as their fmelling Bottle. 'Tis alfo a great Promoter of Mirth, for I have known one *fingle* F A R T, that made an Efcape, raife a Laugh of half an Hour; and the Celebrated Author of a Book, called, *Laugh and Be Fat*, proves Laughing to be a very wholefome Exercife. Dr. *Blow* in his Treatife of the Fundiment-alls of Mufick afferts, that the firft Difcovery of Harmony was owing to an Obfervation of Perfons of different Sizes founding different Notes in Mufick, by Farting; for while one *farted* in *B fa bimi*, another was obferved to anfwer in *F faut*, and make that agreable Concord call'd a *fifth*, whence that Mufical Part had its Name of *Bum-fiddle*, and the firft Invention of the *Double Curtell* was owing to this Obfervation: By this *Rule* it would be an eafy Matter to form a *Farting* Confort, by ranging Perfons of different Sizes in Order, as you would a Ring of Bells, or a Sett of Organ Pipes, which Entertainment would prove much more Diverting round a Tea Table, than the ufual one of Scandal, fince the fweeteft Harmony is allow'd to proceed from the G U T S. Then that Lady will be reckoned the moft agreeable in Company, who is the readieft at *Reportee*; and, to have a good *Report* behind her *Back* would be allow'd a *Strong* Argument of her Merit.

Having thus explained the many Benefits that will attend a Free Practice of F A R T I N G. I think I need ufe no other Arguments to the Ladies, fince their own Eafe, Intereft, and Diverfion plead in its Favour. I fhall therefore *Wind up my Bottom*, and conclude.

We've often heard how the imprifon'd Wind,
When in the Bowels of the Earth confin'd,
And wanting Vent, whate'er refifts, it tears,
And overturns what th' Earth above it bears,

Whole

Whole Towns and People in the wide Rupture fall,
Tho' one fmall Vent, at firft, had fav'd them all,

   So in the Microcofm of Man, we find,
The like ill Fate attends a FART confin'd ;
For Cholick, Vapours, Spleen and Melancholy
Do wreck thofe who fupprefs it, for their Folly.

Hence learn what great Effects fmall things produce.
The Capitol was fav'd from taking by a Goofe.
Then don't admire that one fmall whiffling F A R T
Can guard from Spleen the Citadel your Heart.
And though a Goofe, let me in Time perfuade you,
To guard from Foes, which do behind invade you,
That being of fuch appris'd, you may prepare,
With Speed to plant your ROARING CANNONS there.